CHUCK THE ROOSTER LOSES HIS VOICE

BY SIGAL HABER

WRITTEN BY : SIGAL HABER
ILLUSTRATED BY : AMRIT TIGGA

ENGLISH EDITOR: R. BERMAN

Copyright © 2016 by Sigal Haber
All rights reserved. This book or any portion thereof may not be reproduced or used in any manner whatsoever without the express written permission of the publisher except for the use of brief quotations in a book review.

First Edition, 2016

To My Dear Family

**And to you, where ever you are,
who constantly wakes everyone
in the morning at home**

With Love

Life on the farm has lately been bleak.
It's Chuck the Rooster: He's been sick for a week.
His call has grown soft and his voice is weak
and yesterday by the third crow
he could barely open his beak.

"What happened to him?" the animals wondered.
The rumors gathered like thunder.
"He is getting no better," mournful cries came,
"He needs some help, oh what a shame!"

Some friends were slow to wake again.
The Cow mooed: "I woke late to be milked;
I was late out of bed"
And the Donkey brayed:
"I was late hauling the load ahead!"
The Ewe and Goat never left the pen.
And the mail-bearing Stag, rising late,
was suddenly forced to accelerate.

"My skin got dry and I ran to the mud
to keep from itching," the Pig snorted.
"It's terribly dangerous,
I was woken by the cat," the Mouse retorted.
The fireflies were worried, their faces tight;
they were too late in putting out the light:
"We must switch off the power till night."

The call went out to bring Doctor Owl,
who closely examined the suffering fowl.
Chuck did not look hale, his red crest was pale.
His plumage and wings drooped low
and despair was plainly written on his brow
"It's a clear sign of his state," said his mate.

"Doctor owl," came the weak croaking
as Chuck at his crop with wing was poking.

The owl hushed him, like he already knew
and ordered: "beak open wide!"

The exam results were long overdue
and outside among the animals the tensions grew.
When the doctor left the mews, he told them the news:
"His vocal chords are simply worn out.
Waking everyone up is a chore, no doubt.

Chuck just needs some time off
and I'm also prescribing something for his cough."
Harsh words were said and panic spread:
"Rest! That, sir, is a joke!
Who will make sure that at sunrise we've woke?"

"Ladies and gentlemen," the lizard did rise
We must, all together, a solution devise
and before you all shout, please let me advise."
He quickly climbed on a tall bale of hay
raised his head, and so did he bray:

"A singing competition – that is our mission!"

"Let all of our friends be stand up and heard
and the winner of the most votes will wake the herd
and if I may, I do so say
This is a great opportunity for every Jim Jack or Bob
to add some variety to your old daily job."

The animals fell silent. This was a riddle to solve.
"Competition? Singing? Pray, what does it involve?"

Suddenly the bee sprang into motion:
"A singing contest? What a wonderful notion!
I do love to sing, alone or with choir."
"Moo good," said the cow,
"I've a strong voice, to sing and not tire."
"Meh meh meh provides a steady beat,"
said the sheep,
"both happy and sad kinds of songs I can bleat."
The horses were delighted: "Count us in!
Our galloping, neigh-borly tune's sure to win!"

The dog then barked: "woof woof!
My rocking style will blow off the roof."
"Not sure about that," in reply wailed the Cat,
"seems to me-eeow that you'll just be a goof."
The hen-house was bedlam;
all the chickens squawked and screeched
It was clear that no agreement could be reached.
"Why don't we sleep on it?" Rose the cry in the shed.
"No time for that," the impatient lizard said,
"for by morning the winner must get us all out of bed."

And the skunk on the side said nearly crying:
"Life isn't fair, you know I'm not lying.
If the contest was centered on skill of smell,
there is surely no doubt that I'd do very well."

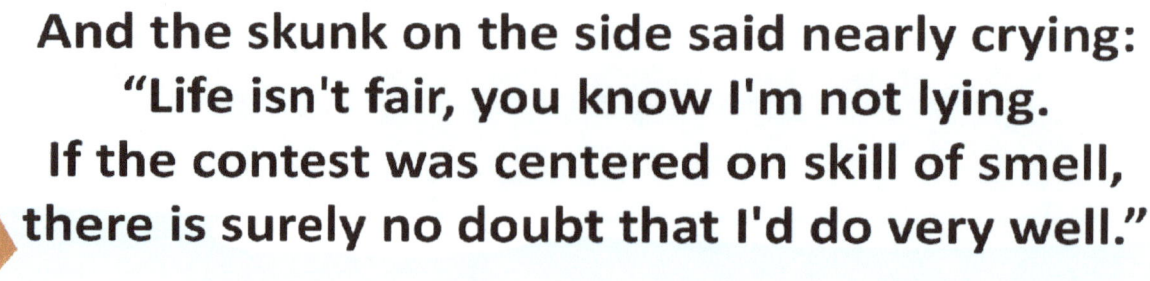

The nimble lizard a list composed
of every participant and the song they chose.
"This," he told them, "is how it will go:
One by one you will come and put on a show.
The crooner whose song will the most praises reap
will as of tomorrow wake us all from our sleep."

All in the farm were very enthused,
to such a good show they had never been used.

"Who will win the prize? Will there be a surprise?"
Said MC Lizard out loud.
"Stay tuned," he added, to the cheers of the crowd.

Behind the tall bale of hay, which now was a stage,
the excitement crackled and curiosity raged.
The dog barked, scaring the goat
who was just then trying to clear her throat.
The duck quacked D sharp and B flat
and wailing at the mic was the feline Miss Cat.

But unexpected problems the production immersed:
The donkey insisted that he should go first.
Lizard was angry: "that's not the right lineup"
And the cow said "Let's move,
I haven't eaten since sun-up."
The sheep was hot for she hadn't been shorn
The bees were all droning and looked quite forlorn.
The hens still hadn't chosen
who would be the chanteuse
The horses were tired and demanded fresh shoes.
And the pig? He was tired, he'd missed his nap
and thought to himself: I'm the wrong sort of chap.
I'm no kind of singer, I can't even rap!"

Meanwhile in the coop,
Chuck the rooster drank tea and ate soup
with some herbs for his throat
and all wrapped in a coat.
And right by his side, his ever-loving bride,
told him all about the song competition.
She was worried about him and about his condition:

"To cry cock-a-doodle each morning is a challenge but this is a task not one other can manage. You are still young and your future is bright. You just need to relax and make sure you live right."

Chuck nodded for he fully agreed,
and asked: "A singing contest? Whatever the need?
Just because someone's sick that's no cause for uproar.
Tell them I'm coming, with an announcement in store."

And just as Lizard was ready to go
and tell everyone that he's stopping the show,
Chuck with his tea climbed the tall bale of hay.
Everyone backstage was surprised, they confessed
and Lizard warmly greeted the guest,
who might unexpectedly save the day.

"Dear friends," grinned lizard, like a seasoned host,
"A quick change in plans, a few moments at most."
He briefly fell silent, then said with great pluck:
"Please welcome our veteran rooster Chuck!"
The audience, astonished, was very excited.
"He's recovered," they chanted, in joy united.

Chuck took the mic and proclaimed:

"Dear friends, I am glad you all came
to play this new and wonderful game.
I've had a rough time, and I'm sorry
if this has caused any trouble or worry."

He sipped from his tea and said, his voice calm:
"Today I've seen how we work arm in arm;
we each have a talent, our own special charm,
which makes us important here on the farm.
It is my duty to do my best
to stay healthy and get plenty of rest.
Come morning, as always, I'll call at sunrise,
and if my voice is not right, don't criticize.
Please understand, it should be no surprise."

"Way to go! Bravo!" rose all over the cries.
His faithful mate, elated at his state,
smiled through tears of joy in her eyes.

"And I hereby announce the annual competition. We'll call it "Farm Idol," and to join the tradition sign up with me, I'll head the commission."

The animals each went their own way.
It had been ages since the farm saw such a day.

Only the dog was disappointed,
he was sure he'd be anointed
He had no doubt his hit, 'Woof Woof'
would have totally brought down the roof

This book had been created with joy and love
Thank you for purchasing it. I hope you enjoyed it.
Your thoughts mean a lot to me.
Please share them with me in my Amazon page :

http://www.amazon.com/-/e/B01BPHFNYY?ref_=pe_1724030_132998070

www.ingramcontent.com/pod-product-compliance
Lightning Source LLC
Chambersburg PA
CBHW050407180526
45159CB00005B/2178